F for the Bus

Peter Corey

Illustrated by Caroline Hu

A Harcourt Achieve Imprint

www.Rigby.com
1-800-531-5015

Literacy by Design Leveled Readers: *Running for the Bus*

ISBN-13: 978-1-4189-3922-9
ISBN-10:   1-4189-3922-6

Printed in China
5 6 7 8 0940 14 13 12 11 10

Contents

Chapter One
Late Again! 5

Chapter Two
Ideas in Writing, Please 12

Chapter Three
A Total Washout 17

Chapter Four
One-on-one 21

Chapter Five
On the Run...27

Chapter Six
Sporting Dreams 35

Chapter Seven
What an Afternoon! 42

Chapter Eight
Into Overdrive...48

Chapter Nine
Fun Running and Fund-raising.................55

Chapter Ten
The New Wheelie.......................................60

Chapter One
Late Again!

"STOP! Pleeeeeaaase stoooop!"

Waving his lunchbox and shouting, Tommy Tyler ran down the street as fast as he could, desperately trying to catch up with the school bus as it pulled away from the curb. Tommy's heart pounded as loud as a drum. He waved his arms high over his head, but it didn't make any difference.

A few blocks ahead, the bus slowed down, giving Tommy a small bit of hope. But just as he started running again, the left turn signal came on, the bus made the turn, and that hope was gone in a cloud of dust.

Tommy's face glowed as red as a stop sign. Bent over with his hands on his knees, he struggled to catch his breath.

Tommy knew then that it was hopeless. He might be able to catch his breath, but he'd never catch the bus now. For the zillionth time, the driver hadn't seen him, and the bus had taken off without him. Beads of sweat ran down Tommy's face as he crumbled, breathless, onto the grass beside the sidewalk.

"It's not fair," he panted.

Tommy was the shortest kid in his class, and some of his classmates even called him "Shorty," which he hated.

"If I were taller, I'd be able to run faster," he told himself. "If I were taller, the driver would see me and wouldn't drive off. Being short is the worst!"

But the one thing that was worse than missing the bus was being late for school. He imagined what his teacher, Mr. Stevens, would say when he finally did get to school: "Late again, Tommy? You really should buy yourself an alarm clock."

How could he explain to somebody as merciless as Mr. Stevens that being late had nothing to do with his alarm clock and everything to do with the fact that his bus driver had a hard time seeing short people?

Not to mention the fact that his home was a madhouse in the mornings! Mom and Dad were always rushing to get ready for work. Baby sister Sara had to be fed, and because she had just started teething, she was always crying. It was a nightmare! But how could he explain any of that to "Strict Stevens," who was probably never late?

One thing he was certain about, though, was that if he didn't get up off this grass and get to school, he'd be really late, and then Strict Stevens would be stricter than ever.

Tommy wiped the last of the sweat off his forehead with his sleeve. Then he got up and dusted the grass off his clothes. He patted the top of his hair to make sure it still looked right. He always wore it spiked in the front, hoping that it made him look taller.

As he quickly gathered up his backpack and lunchbox, he heard a familiar voice shout, "Tom, my man! Do you know anything at all about broken-down buses?"

Tommy looked over and saw the smiling face of his best friend Adam, who was speeding toward him in his bright red wheelchair.

"Looks like we're *both* going to be late for school today," Adam said, grinning happily.

"Why is that?" Tommy asked.

"Because the minibus we take has quit working again. It's broken down so much lately that I can't remember the last time we made it to school on time!" Adam joked. "Oh well, we'll just get on with it!"

Just get on with it was Adam's favorite saying. It meant that he had a carefree attitude toward the kinds of things that Tommy really stressed out about. Tommy often wondered why nothing ever really bothered Adam. There was a lot he could learn from his friend.

Glancing back down the road, he spotted Adam's minibus, the one that carried the kids with wheelchairs to school. There were ten kids in all, and they called themselves the *Wheelies*. Just like Adam, none of the other Wheelies seemed to mind that their transportation had broken down.

The hood of the minibus was open, and a mixture of smoke and steam was snaking up from the engine. The driver scratched his head in confusion and spoke into his cell phone to the school principal, Mrs. Knowles.

"Sorry, Mrs. Knowles," the driver said, holding the phone in a hand covered in engine grease. "It's gone for good. But don't you worry. I'll get these kids to school safe and sound."

Tommy watched as the driver ran around like a crazy sheepdog trying to herd his flock of Wheelies. He called after them, "You kids better get into a crocodile and make it snappy!"

Tommy wasn't really sure what that was supposed to mean, but at least he forgot about his own troubles for a moment as he struggled not to laugh. Then, checking his watch, he called to Adam, "I have to go! I'm going to be really late!"

"You know," Adam said, rubbing his chin playfully, "there's a spare wheelchair in the back of the minibus. I bet it'd get you to school in half the time."

"Awesome!" Tommy said.

He quickly snatched the spare wheelchair from where it was stored, but by the time he'd opened it, sat down, and worked out how to steer the thing, the Wheelies had gone. Tommy had been left in the dust for the second time that morning.

The Wheelies were about a block up the road with the driver running after them, breathlessly trying to keep up.

"Hey, you guys, wait!" Tommy and the driver both shouted, but the Wheelies ignored them and disappeared around the corner.

Balancing his lunchbox and backpack on his knees, Tommy gripped the wheels of the chair and started pushing himself slowly up the hill.

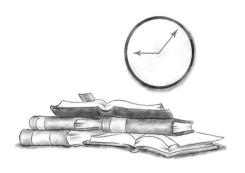

Chapter Two
Ideas in Writing, Please

Mr. Stevens didn't seem to notice Tommy slip into class half an hour later. He was too busy reading a note from the principal.

Mr. Stevens first read the note to himself, a thoughtful expression on his face. When he was finished, he put his thick-rimmed reading glasses back into his jacket pocket.

"If I could have your attention, please," Mr. Stevens said, and everyone in the class stopped what they were doing.

"Mrs. Knowles has informed me that the minibus used to transport our children with disabilities has gone its last mile," Mr. Stevens told them. "This means that until a replacement vehicle can be purchased, those students will be unable to attend school."

The class exploded into chaos and noise. Some cried, "No fair!" Others agreed with Mrs. Knowles, and still others muttered comments like "lucky ducks!"

Mr. Stevens raised his hands to shush the class. "Because of this, Mrs. Knowles has asked for *helpful* suggestions for fund-raising so that the school may purchase a new minibus."

This time the class started buzzing with excited chatter, so Mr. Stevens held up his hands again and said, "Let's not discuss it now. Any ideas should be written—*neatly*—on a sheet of paper and given to the principal on Monday for review."

A short time later, the bell sounded for the end of the class period, and everyone headed for the door. Tommy tried to sneak out by blending in with a clump of his classmates, but Mr. Stevens spotted him.

"Ah, Mr. Tyler," Mr. Stevens called in a stern tone. "May I see you for a moment?"

Fully expecting to be thrown into detention for the rest of his life, Tommy shuffled up to the teacher's desk with the speed of a snail.

But instead of sending Tommy to detention, Mr. Stevens said, "So good of you to join us today, Tommy—and just in time for your next class period, too. Try not to be quite so late tomorrow. Now run along."

Tommy didn't need to be told twice! He'd somehow escaped punishment, so he bolted from the classroom as fast as lightning, wondering why he hadn't gotten into trouble. That was the problem with teachers, Tommy decided. You could never quite tell what they were thinking.

At lunch that day in the cafeteria, the whole school was talking about fund-raising ideas, many of which Tommy thought weren't very good. But as he bit into his sandwich, the only thing going through his head was, *I haven't got a single idea, not even a really bad one!*

"What am I going to do?" Tommy asked Adam when they met up on the playground after lunch. "I want to help raise money for you guys to get a new minibus, but I can't think of anything."

"The Wheelies are holding a Bask-a-Thon," Adam told him. "You could do something like that."

"What's a Bask-a-Thon?"

"It's a Wild Wheelies basketball game. We sell tickets, and all the money goes toward the new minibus."

"Cool!" exclaimed Tommy. "Count me in. I'm pretty good at basketball!"

"We'd love to have you play, buddy, but there's only one problem," Adam said as he pointed to Tommy's legs.

"Why? What's wrong with my legs?" Tommy asked.

"You're not in a wheelchair. I'm sorry, but this is a Wheelie basketball game."

"Oh, I see," Tommy said, trying to hide his disappointment.

"I know what you can do! You can help me get into shape," Adam suggested. "Let's shoot some baskets at my place after school on Monday. I bet Mom will even feed you. Deal?"

"You got it!" Tommy said excitedly. They sealed the deal with a high five, just as the bell sounded for the next period.

Tommy watched his friend wheel himself toward his next class, thinking how much he was looking forward to shooting baskets with Adam on Monday. It was now Friday, so he only had two days to wait. He also only had two days to come up with his own fund-raising idea, and at the moment, he didn't have a clue about what he was going to do.

Chapter Three
A Total Washout

That Saturday over breakfast, Tommy discussed the problem with his family.

"What about a bake sale?" his mother suggested, trying to be helpful.

"He'd end up eating more than he sold," his father laughed, being very unhelpful.

"Yoo goo gaa gaa," baby Sara added, trying to speak.

"Thanks," said Tommy, wishing he'd never asked them.

As he took his cereal bowl to the sink to rinse it out, his father asked, "What about washing cars? I bet plenty of people would pay five dollars or more to have their car washed. I know I would."

"That's a great idea! Thanks, Dad," said Tommy.

"At least, I would if my car was dirty," Dad added.

There goes that five bucks, Tommy thought.

"But I'm sure Mr. Dent next door would pay you to wash his car—if it was for charity," Mom suggested.

As far as Tommy could tell, Mr. Dent was not the sort of man who was easy to please, even if it was for a good cause. He wanted everything perfect. His clothes were perfectly clean, the grass in his yard was perfectly cut, and the trees around his house were perfectly trimmed. And besides, Mr. Dent's car was always spotless. Would he even need a car wash? Still, *anything* was worth a try.

"I have to do this right," Tommy told himself as he made a big cardboard sign that said: *Car Wash—$5—For Chatary.*

"Five dollars? That sounds like a lot of money," Mr. Dent complained when Tommy approached him later that afternoon.

"But it's for charity," Tommy told him, hoping for the best.

"Really? Your sign says *'chatary'*." Mr. Dent pointed out that *charity* was misspelled on the sign.

Spelling had never been Tommy's best subject, which was why he hadn't signed up for the fund-raising Spell-a-Thon. Tommy explained that the school was trying to raise enough money to buy a new minibus for the Wheelies.

Mr. Dent grunted, "OK, but it better be spotless. I want to be able to see my face in it."

It took only about ten minutes for Tommy to discover that getting a car clean was no big deal, but getting it spotless was something else! No matter how many buckets of water he threw on it, as soon as the water dried in the sun, dirty spots appeared. In the end Tommy decided to give the spots a quick wipe and hope that they didn't reappear before Mr. Dent approved the work.

He dropped his sponge into his bucket and rang Mr. Dent's doorbell.

"You call that spotless?" Mr. Dent said, after he had examined every inch of the car like a policeman looking for clues.

"Well . . ." Tommy began, but Mr. Dent stopped him with a shake of his head.

"There's no way I'm paying five green ones for that—not even for *chatary*!"

All that work for nothing, Tommy thought. He decided that trying to fund-raise by washing cars was pointless.

Chapter Four
One-on-one

Tommy almost didn't go to Adam's house after school that Monday. The day had started badly enough as it was. He'd missed the bus—*again*. It had gone downhill fast from there, especially since Tommy had to sit in class, listening to everyone bragging about how much money they would raise.

"Hey, Tom, where you going?" Adam called as Tommy left school that afternoon.

"Home," Tommy told him.

"No way! You're coming back to my house. It's all arranged! Mom's making your favorite dinner and . . . by the way, what is your favorite dinner?"

"Pizza," Tommy told him.

"Well in that case, Mom's got *my* favorite dinner planned!" Then Adam put on a pleading voice and pretended to beg. "You've got to help me train!"

Tommy chuckled at his friend as they headed off to Adam's house. An hour later the two boys were in the middle of a very uneven game of one-on-one. Adam was an amazing basketball player. His wheelchair whizzed around the court like a bee around honey. The best Tommy could do was stand and guard the basket, but Adam still had plenty of easy shots. In fact, if Adam hadn't kept missing the basket on purpose, the game would have been a total blowout.

Luckily, the game was cut short when Adam's mother called to them through the kitchen window. "Pasta's ready!"

"OK, so it's not *pizza*," Adam confessed, "but at least they both begin with *P*. What more do you want?" And with that, Adam disappeared into the house. Tommy followed, thankful that the game was over.

As they ate their dinner, Tommy had a question he was dying to ask. He wasn't going to at first, but then, casting a glance to Adam's chair, he nervously asked, "What's it like . . . ?"

Adam finished the question for him. "What's it like being in a wheelchair?" Tommy nodded, and Adam looked thoughtful for a few seconds. He said, laughing, "Eating pasta's better!"

Adam went on to explain: "It's not good or bad. It's just the way things are. I just get on with it and never look back."

The two boys ate in silence for a while, and Tommy felt humbled by Adam's courage. He could never see Adam getting stressed about something like being short, as Tommy himself had. It made Tommy even more determined to help his friend improve his basket-shooting skills.

"Oh! I didn't tell you," Adam suddenly blurted out, almost causing Tommy to choke on his pasta. "Mrs. Knowles has given the Wheelies the rest of the week off from school!"

"Why would she do that?" Tommy asked.

Adam made a silly face. "Duh! No bus, no way of getting to school." Then he leaned close and whispered so no one else could hear. "If you could get a few days off school, too, we could get in some serious basketball practice!"

"I'm sure Tommy's parents would have something to say about that!" Adam's mom commented as she brought over two bowls of ice cream.

"Oh well," said Adam, smirking. "I'll be thinking about you poor guys in school while I'm watching TV all day!"

"Think again, young man," his mother said, causing Adam's smirk to disappear completely from his face. "Some of the parents have kindly agreed to give you guys a ride to school."

"WHAT?" Adam nearly spilled his ice cream.

"They've worked out a schedule, and I'm on it. So, not only will you be going to school tomorrow, but I'll be taking you!" And with that, Adam's mom kissed the top of his head and took the dirty plates away.

While Adam shook out his mop of black hair, as though trying to get the kiss out of it, Tommy said, "Your *mom's* taking you to school? That's so not cool!"

"I know, I'll never live it down!" Adam agreed, but then almost instantly, he was back to his cheery self again. "But we can still practice every day after school, right?"

"You bet!" agreed Tommy, and they gave it their usual high five.

Adam's mother picked them both up from school every afternoon that week, and they went back to Adam's house to shoot hoops together. With Tommy's help, Adam learned to slow down long enough to take a calm and careful shot at the basket. When he took his time, Adam made more baskets than when he rushed or just threw the ball at the backboard.

Tommy was an excellent coach, and Adam was very grateful for the help. In fact, Tommy's coaching gave Adam an idea.

"Why don't you set up a charity basketball game with some non-Wheelies?" he suggested. "You're plenty good enough."

"Yeah, but I'm not plenty tall enough!" Tommy explained.

"That's true," Adam joked. "They'd keep stepping on you, Shorty!"

Tommy laughed, then he snatched the ball from his friend's hands and drove it into the basket for two points.

Chapter Five
On the Run

Every morning that next week, Tommy ran as fast as he could to catch the bus.

On Monday he missed it, which was usual for a Monday.

On Tuesday he missed it, but just barely.

On Wednesday he *caught* the bus, but just barely.

On Thursday he caught it with plenty of time to spare, which was almost unheard of.

On Friday he found himself standing at the bus stop, but there was no bus to be seen. "What happened to the bus?" Tommy asked another kid who was also waiting. "Is it late?"

"No," the kid told him, "you're early."

"I'm *what*?"

Tommy couldn't even remember the last time he'd been early for the bus. The more he ran, the faster he was getting. If he kept on training like this, he might eventually be able to outrun the bus completely. He'd like to see the look on the bus driver's face then!

All this talk about running and training gave him an idea. If he could run for the bus and catch it, then surely he could run to raise money for the new Wheelie bus.

That was it! That was the something he was good at! So what if he was the shortest kid in class? He wasn't going to let that stop him. First thing Monday morning, he would put his name down for the charity Fun Run. All he had to do was find some people to sponsor him, and then they would pay for every lap around the track he ran. It was perfect!

That evening during basketball practice, he told Adam his plan. But instead of looking excited, it made his friend look really upset.

"I guess that means you won't have time to help me practice my three-point shots anymore," Adam said.

Tommy felt horrible. He'd promised to help Adam, and he couldn't back out of that. "Of course I will! I'll make time to . . . "

"Just kidding!" Adam laughed. "I know you'd never let me down. Just make sure you get plenty of running practice. If you're going to be in the Fun Run, I want you to raise the most money of all."

"I will," Tommy said. "I'll start right now. In fact, I'll run everywhere I go!"

When Tommy said "everywhere," he really meant it. He started by running home that evening. Then, for the whole weekend, he ran every place he went. He even ran around the house, which nearly drove his parents up the wall.

"That kid's gone crazy!" Mother complained over breakfast one morning, just after Tommy had run through with his lunchbox. "He's running from one end of the house to the other!"

"I know," Dad agreed. "It's like living in the middle of a soccer game!"

"Meep meep!" said baby Sara.

The next morning Dad was grabbing a quick cup of coffee before work, just as he was also trying to stuff an important report into his briefcase. He'd stayed up half the night getting the report finished, but as soon as he'd printed one copy, the computer had crashed and wouldn't turn back on. To make things worse, this morning the whole family was running late, as usual, and Mom couldn't find a matching pair of socks for Sara to wear.

Just then, Tommy came running through the middle of the kitchen like a small tornado.

He wasn't watching where he was going, and he crashed right into Dad, sending a shower of coffee down his suit and all over his report. Dad cried out in pain from the hot coffee, causing Sara to burst into tears. He was dripping wet and his report was ruined.

"It's OK, don't worry," Mom said, wiping coffee off Dad's suit. "Just go back upstairs and print another copy of your report."

"I can't. The computer's still down."

Dad bent down on one knee in front of Tommy. "Son," he began, "all of this running has got to stop. Someone's going to get hurt. Someone besides just me."

This made Sara's tears turn into cheerful giggles.

"But, Dad . . . " Tommy started to say.

"Son," Dad said sternly. "From now on you walk everywhere. OK? Everywhere."

And with that, Dad picked up his briefcase and wet report and went off to work.

Tommy turned to his mother for support, pleading, "But Mom, I've got to keep running! If I want to be good enough to do the Fun Run, then I've got to build up my . . . what do you call it?"

"Stamina?" Mom suggested.

"That's it! And I can't build up my stamina without lots of running."

Mom rested her hand on Tommy's arm and said, "I do understand, dear, but you heard your father."

"But what if I'm not in shape for the Fun Run?" Tommy cried.

His mother gave him a peck on the cheek. "I think that if you just didn't run around the house, then . . . "

"But Dad said I've got to walk *everywhere*!" Tommy said.

"Yes, I know. But you do understand why we're worried, don't you? It's not safe to be running around the house like you've been, especially with your little sister learning to crawl."

"I understand, Mom. Sorry," Tommy said, then he picked up his backpack and lunchbox and left the house—*walking*.

The bus was coming, and Tommy realized that if he kept on walking, he would miss it for sure. However, if he ran, he'd be in trouble with his parents. But at the same time, if he missed the bus, he'd be in trouble with Mr. Stevens. He was between a rock and a hard place, and he didn't know what to do. He thought everything over carefully and then made a decision.

He ran for the bus.

Chapter Six
Sporting Dreams

Tommy not only ran for the bus—he kept right on running. He passed the bus, ran all the way to school, and then started running laps around the track. In fact, he ran for three days straight, nonstop, and he'd barely even broken a sweat! Not only that, he burned out the bottoms of two pairs of shoes and drank 56 gallons of water.

Other runners had joined in along the way, but they had no chance of keeping up. Before long, all of them had hit the ground with exhaustion, and Tommy wasn't even out of breath. With every lap the total amount of money he'd raised in the Fun Run was chalked up on a board. Tommy was just passing the three-million-dollar mark when the principal told him to stop.

Tommy felt that he could have easily kept on running forever, but why show off? After all, he'd already raised enough money to buy a whole fleet of solid-gold minibuses with wings and rocket engines. Tommy figured he had done more than enough, so as he coasted past the finish line for the last time, he decided to take a break. As he crossed the line, everyone was cheering, even the teachers.

Tommy was the coolest guy in school!

Mr. Stevens came up to shake the hand of the hero who'd saved the day, but when Tommy reached out to take it, Mr. Stevens shook his shoulder instead.

"Good morning, Tommy . . . "

And with that, Tommy woke from his daydream. He was back in his desk in Mr. Stevens's classroom. All of his classmates were staring at him and chuckling. Mr. Stevens towered over him, arms folded across his chest.

"I was so pleased when you arrived on time for school this morning," Mr. Stevens said, "but what a pity you've ruined it by falling asleep in class. If you can manage to stay awake, please report to the principal's office during recess."

He had to go to the principal's office? He'd never been sent there in all the time he'd been in school! There was no telling what went on there, but he'd heard stories about kids who'd gone in and never came back out again.

Tommy tried to tell himself that they were only stories. *They were only stories. They were only stories. No need to panic, right?*

As he waited nervously outside the office, he thought about running away. After all, he was pretty good at running now. But it was too late. The principal's secretary stood over him like a prison guard.

"Off you go," the secretary said. "Mrs. Knowles is ready for you now."

Taking a deep breath, Tommy knocked on the door very softly, hoping that maybe Mrs. Knowles wouldn't hear. That way he could leave and pretend that she wasn't there. But Tommy knew that principals, like teachers, could hear *everything*—even soft knocking.

"Come in!" said the voice from the other side of the door. Tommy slowly turned the knob and went in.

"Have a seat, dear. I won't bite," said Mrs. Knowles, trying to make a joke. But Tommy wasn't in much of a laughing mood. He was far too scared.

"Mr. Stevens tells me that you fell asleep during his class this morning. That's not like you at all, Tommy. You're not usually *here* for his class."

Mrs. Knowles smiled at her second little joke, which made Tommy wonder if this was part of her plan. She'd make a few jokes, get him relaxed, then send him to detention for life.

"Mr. Stevens also tells me that you've signed up for the Fun Run. I think that's great, but you won't run very far if you're asleep, will you?"

Tommy didn't know if he was supposed to answer this or not, so he said nothing.

"Believe it or not, I happen to know a thing or two about running," Mrs. Knowles said. She pointed to a cabinet in the corner of her office. "Go on. Open the door."

Afraid of what might be hiding behind those heavy wooden doors, Tommy cautiously lifted the latch that held the cabinet shut. As he started to open it, he caught sight of his reflection in the shiny wood—he looked *terrified*! He swung the doors open and saw . . . small silver trophies. There were about a dozen altogether, some of them dull and dirty with age and a lack of cleaning.

"They're for running mostly, but a few are for swimming. The swimming trophies are the ones that need the most cleaning," Mrs. Knowles said. "So, now you see, Tommy. Believe me when I say that I know a few things about sports training."

Tommy looked at her as she smiled at him, and he realized that he'd never noticed how short she was. She wasn't much taller than him, in fact.

He found himself smiling at the thought of the school principal actually running anywhere, and Mrs. Knowles noticed his smile.

"That's better," she said. "Now, let's talk about getting you ready for the Fun Run."

Tommy told her all about helping Adam, and how angry his father had been about him running around the house. Mrs. Knowles seemed to know exactly what he was talking about.

"My father used to get angry with me, too. But the trouble is that when you discover something you're good at, you just want to do it all the time."

"Exactly!" Tommy cried, amazed that she understood.

Mrs. Knowles seemed to read his thoughts. "Believe it or not, teachers were children once, too—even school principals like me!"

Tommy was struggling to imagine this when Mrs. Knowles told him, "I'm glad that you've decided to help your friend, but maybe you need a little help, too. If your parents agree, how would you like some running practice after school? It'll build up your . . . "

"Stamina?" Tommy blurted out.

"Exactly," Mrs. Knowles said, beaming at him.

"I'd really like that, but . . . "

Mrs. Knowles held up her hand. "Leave it all to me. You just be on the track ready to go right after school this afternoon."

Even though Tommy was glad to get out of the principal's office, he was actually looking forward to his training session after school that day. The only thing he was struggling to get his mind around was the idea of Mrs. Knowles running. He kept imagining her in a bright pink tracksuit, which made it very hard for him to concentrate that afternoon.

It was Mr. Stevens who brought him back to reality. "Just because you're training after school, Tommy, doesn't mean that you don't have to pay attention in class. Your training session can be canceled just as easily as it was arranged, you know."

"Sorry," Tommy said. He didn't want to miss training with the principal, even if she did turn up in a bright pink tracksuit!

Chapter Seven
What an Afternoon!

As soon as the bell rang at the end of school, Tommy rushed to the locker room, changed into his running shorts and shoes, and headed for the running track. Calling it a "running track" was actually being nice, as it was really only the outside edge of the school playground that had been marked up for running—not that anybody used it very much for running.

But as Adam would say, he should just "get on with it." And that's exactly what Tommy intended to do.

Mrs. Knowles was already at the track waiting for him. Tommy was surprised to see that she was still wearing her usual dress suit and heels. Surely she wasn't going to try and run in those!

Mrs. Knowles must have realized what he was thinking because she greeted him with, "Did you think *I* was going to be running with you? Absolutely not! Can you imagine me wearing something like a bright pink tracksuit?" Then she laughed out loud.

Although Tommy shared the laugh, he was secretly thinking, *You have no idea!*

"No, Tommy, swimming was always more my sport, which used to drive my father crazy. He was terrified of water, you see." Mrs. Knowles pointed off into the distance. "That's your coach over there. He's the runner."

Tommy looked to where she was pointing and saw someone in a tracksuit and running shoes a short distance away. Whoever this person was, he was busy stretching and warming up.

"Give him a few minutes to warm up. He's a little rusty," Mrs. Knowles said. And with that, she walked back into the school, leaving Tommy to wonder who his coach could be.

Tommy's new coach was bent over with his back toward Tommy, which meant that he couldn't see his coach's face. Who could he be?

Just then, Tommy heard a familiar voice behind him.

"Hey, Shorty, you still helping me with my basketball practice?" Adam asked.

Oh no! Tommy had forgotten all about practicing with Adam, who was coming toward him right now. This was going to be tricky!

Adam glanced over at the guy doing stretches and asked, "Who's the guy in the funny tracksuit . . . Oh hi, Mr. Stevens!"

Mr. Stevens, thought Tommy. *No way!*

"I think you'll find that Tommy has other plans this evening, Adam," Mr. Stevens said stiffly.

"Cool, no problem," said Adam. Then turning back to Tommy, he smiled a huge smile and added, "Have fun!"

Fun was the last thing Tommy felt like having right now. He felt terrible. Not only had he let Adam down, but he was going to be training with Strict Stevens. Could life get any worse?

To Tommy's surprise, instead of getting worse, things actually started to go pretty well. The training session with Mr. Stevens turned out to be really helpful, and although he never completely loosened up, Mr. Stevens was much friendlier than he'd ever been in class.

However, Mrs. Knowles had been right about him being "a little rusty." He wasn't in quite as good a shape as he'd been when he was Tommy's age, he admitted.

It was during one of their many "breathers" that Mr. Stevens told Tommy about his time as a runner. He'd been quite successful and even had trophies to prove it. They were the ones in the principal's cabinet. What Tommy hadn't known was that Mrs. Knowles kept them because she was Mr. Stevens's aunt!

"I even dreamed of one day running in the Olympics," Mr. Stevens told him.

"What happened?" Tommy asked.

"I woke up," Mr. Stevens replied.

For a split second, he looked sad and thoughtful, but then he quickly changed the subject. "I think that's enough running for one day. Make sure that you practice those breathing exercises I taught you."

And with that, Mr. Stevens turned away and walked briskly back into the school building.

Tommy called after him, "Um, thanks, Mr. Stevens." But his new coach had already gone.

What an afternoon it had been! Not only had Tommy learned how to breathe when he was running, but he'd also learned that Principal Knowles had been a swimmer and had driven her dad crazy, too; that she was Mr. Stevens's aunt and that the running trophies in her cabinet were his; and that Mr. Stevens had dreamed of one day being in the Olympics. Tommy couldn't wait to tell Adam!

Adam! Tommy came down to Earth with a bump, remembering that he was supposed to be helping Adam train, but instead . . .

Chapter Eight
Into Overdrive

". . . but instead you put yourself first,"
Adam said as Tommy tried to apologize the
following day.

"I'm sorry, man. Really."

"Why should you be sorry?" Adam asked.
"Just because we're pals doesn't mean that you
can't think of yourself, too. You want to do well
in the Fun Run, don't you?"

"Well, yes, but . . . "

"But nothing! Thanks to you, I'm a total
basketball superstar. I never miss!"

They both knew that Adam was
stretching the truth a little, but that didn't
bother Tommy.

"In fact," Adam continued, "I think I owe
you, Tommy, not the other way around. Well,
it's payback time. Now I'm going to help you!"

"How?"

"I can help you count laps," Adam replied.

"You need somebody who can help you keep track of how far you've run."

"You'd do that?" Tommy asked.

"Sure! With me helping, you're going to run so far that your sponsors are going to go broke when they have to pay up!"

Tommy suddenly looked blank, then all the color washed out of his face. "Sponsors?" he asked.

"You do have sponsors, don't you?" Adam asked, but the look on Tommy's face told him everything.

Adam shook his head, laughed, and said, "You're about as much use as a hat rack is to a moose!"

And so, with only a few days to go before the Fun Run that weekend, Tommy's life went into overdrive. When he wasn't training with Adam, he was training with Mr. Stevens. And when he wasn't doing either of those things, he was racing around trying to get relatives, friends, and neighbors to sponsor him.

Even Mr. Dent let Tommy add his name to the list, grumbling, "I'll pay one cent per lap. That should be more than enough."

"Wow, that's very generous," Tommy told him with a strained smile.

"Would you like the ten cents now for the ten laps you're going to run? That way you won't even have to bother!" Mr. Dent chuckled.

"No thanks, Mr. Dent," Tommy told him, "I want to do it properly. After all, it is for . . ."

"Yes, I know . . . *chatary!*"

The day of the Fun Run finally arrived. Actually, it was only the "day of the Fun Run" for the fifty or so students who were taking part in it. For the others it was the "day of the Chess-a-Thon," or the "day of the Spell-a-Thon,"

or the "day of the Quiet Game Challenge."
Pretty much everyone in school was involved in
some sort of activity.

All the events had been arranged for that
Saturday afternoon and set up around the
school. That way they could also sell food and
drinks and hold raffles so they could raise
even more money for the minibus.

For Adam, the day was meant to be the
"day of the Wild Wheelies basketball game,"
but when Tommy found him in the locker
room, it was clear to him that something
was wrong.

"You OK?" Tommy asked, knowing right away what the answer would be.

"No," Adam said sadly. "One of our players hurt his elbow during our practice game yesterday, and we don't know whether he will be able to play or not. At first the doctor said he was fine, then he wasn't fine, then he was again, but now he might not be."

Adam looked worried for the first time ever. "What am I going to do, Tom?" he pleaded.

Tommy thought for a second, then said very gently, "Just . . . get on with it."

There was silence from Adam, which made Tommy realize that this was either the worst thing he could have said, or exactly what Adam needed to hear.

A few seconds ticked by, then a broad smile stretched across Adam's face.

"You know, you're right!" Adam told him cheerfully. "Thanks, Shorty! Now then, let's go and do your Fun Run. I'll worry about the basketball game later."

As Tommy stood on the starting line of the Fun Run, he thought back to the day that the minibus had broken down. It was only about two weeks ago, but it seemed like a lifetime, especially since he'd packed so much into such a short time.

First he'd learned how to run properly. Then he'd learned that it was possible for teachers to surprise you—they had been kids once, too! But most importantly, he'd learned the value of true friendship. Even though he'd been worried about his own fund-raiser, Adam was there on the side of the track, ready to count laps for his friend and cheer him on.

Tommy's family was also there to wish him well.

"Good luck, dear," said Mom. "Be careful."

"Don't forget to breathe," said Dad. "Breathing is important."

"Thanks, Mom. Thanks, Dad."

But the best advice came from baby Sara. "Foo gooby," she told him.

"I'll try," Tommy laughed, not really knowing exactly what she was talking about.

Mr. Stevens was in charge of the run, and he called all the runners to the starting line. Tommy got into position . . . then he started running.

"Tommy, stop! You have to wait for my whistle!" Mr. Stevens called after him.

"Just warming up!" Tommy called back.

"Ah, good idea!" Mr. Stevens said.

Tommy completed his warm-up lap, and as he returned to the rest of the runners, Mr. Stevens blew his whistle and the Fun Run began for real.

Chapter Nine
Fun Running and Fund-raising

The Fun Runners swarmed forward, packed tightly and forcing each other along. Being a "fun" event, the students were allowed to wear homemade costumes. There was a mouse chasing a cat, and someone with bright green hair and skin. Tommy ran past a superhero who was already sweating and out of breath.

The audience really enjoyed the costumes, but most of the outfits were impossible to stand up in, let alone run in! As Tommy tried to free himself from the waving tentacles of a rubber and foam octopus, a cardboard robot staggered past, tripping over his own feet.

After a few laps, some of the runners decided they'd done enough and dropped out, but Tommy was going all the way. What was the point of all that training if he gave up after five minutes?

Besides, the training was really paying off. He was up to ten laps now, and he felt as though he'd only walked a few steps.

But Tommy soon realized that although running round and round the track may be fun to *do*, it wasn't much fun to *watch*. Pretty soon the runners' parents started drifting away to grab some food, talk with friends, or watch the Chess-a-Thon in the school library.

"Thirty-three!" Adam called out as Tommy ran past the checkpoint for the thirty-third time. Tommy was glad Adam was counting for him. It meant that he could concentrate on other things, such as wondering what was happening at the other fund-raising events.

He imagined that at the Spell-a-Thon in the cafeteria, someone had just tried to spell the word *onomatopoeia*. Tommy was grateful that it wasn't him! Meanwhile at the Chess-a-Thon, a pawn had probably just been taken. And at the Quiet Game Challenge in the gym, somebody might have made a joke about not being able to hear anything.

Tommy was really letting his mind wander!

"Fifty!" Adam shouted. "You've gone fifty laps! That's more than twelve miles!"

"That's plenty, dear!" called Tommy's mother. "I think you need to rest!"

I bet she wishes she hadn't agreed to sponsor one dollar a lap! Tommy thought. Even so, he intended to keep going as long as he could, whatever it cost his sponsors. More than anything, he wanted to help his friend Adam and the Wheelies get their new minibus.

By the time he reached lap number sixty, less than half the runners were left. At seventy laps, most of the remaining runners had dropped out. By ninety, there were only a handful still going. Tommy was determined to reach one hundred laps, but by now he was running on autopilot. He was really starting to lose his concentration, and he was getting pretty thirsty.

Adam seemed to sense it. "That's 97 laps! Keep going, Tommy! Don't give up!"

But Tommy wasn't listening. He was running in a daze, feeling light-headed. Adam knew that if his friend was going to make the hundred laps, he would need a little help. And so, Adam started wheeling alongside the track, shouting, "Keep it up, Tommy! You've only got three more laps!"

Suddenly Tommy jolted, as though he was waking up from a dream. He started sprinting so fast that Adam had trouble keeping up. The other runners didn't bother trying to catch up with him. Everyone dropped out, leaving Tommy to run alone.

Word spread like wildfire that Tommy Tyler was going to do one hundred laps. In the gym, Tommy's classmate Fay Westerby blurted out, "One hundred?" Then she realized that she'd just lost the Quiet Game Challenge!

Fans abandoned the Chess-a-Thon just as a knight was moving to take the other player's king. They didn't care. They wanted to see Tommy Tyler cross the finish line on his one hundredth lap.

"Ninety-nine, Tommy!" Adam called out to him. "Keep going!"

Whatever he did, Tommy would not slow down. He was running for the bus, and he meant to get it. Nothing was going to stop him.

Nothing—except maybe a trip, followed by a fall . . .

"Noooooo!" shouted Adam, but Tommy couldn't hear him. He was already unconscious.

Chapter Ten
The New Wheelie

"Can you follow my finger, Tommy?"

All Tommy could think was, *Why? Where's it going?*

He slowly focused until he could see Mr. Stevens crouching over him, moving his finger from left to right. Or was it right to left? Anyway, it was moving. Tommy at least knew that much.

Mr. Stevens was trying to calm everyone else down by saying, "I think he's doing fine . . . "

"My leg hurts."

" . . . except for his leg," Mr. Stevens added, slightly embarrassed.

Mrs. Knowles moved in to have a look. "I don't think there's anything broken, but he may have torn something in his knee." Then to Tommy, she said quietly, "You did it: one hundred laps. Well done!"

"It was only 99," Tommy said weakly.

"Surely you're going to count your warm-up lap. I certainly would," Mrs. Knowles said as she squeezed his hand.

"I'll bring my car around," said Tommy's dad. "We should get him to the hospital."

"Are you thirsty, dear?" Tommy's mom asked. "Would you like some water?"

Adam came up beside him. "How's the leg?"

"It's OK," Tommy said. Then he added, "Eating pasta's better!"

To the surprise of the crowd, the two friends laughed. They were still laughing when Dad finally arrived with the car to take Tommy to the hospital.

"I'll come, too," Adam said.

"No way," Tommy said. "You've got a basketball game to win!"

And that's just what Adam and the Wheelies did. The doctor decided that in the end their hurt player was well enough to play, so the Wheelies had a full team. And they needed it because the other team, the Rockets, was good . . . real good.

At the end of the first period, the score was tied 24 to 24. Thanks to all of Tommy's coaching, Adam had scored 14 of those points. He remembered how it had been playing against his friend back at home after school. And it worked! Adam slowed down and was calm, and he made basket after basket.

With only one minute left in the game, the score was tied again at 62 to 62. The clock ticked, the ball was passed and passed again. A member of the Rocket's team knew Adam was a good shot, so she did everything she could to block Adam out.

Adam rolled left, he rolled right, then he faked left and instead rolled right—and he broke free! He was open!

Another Wheelie passed Adam the ball, he shot, the ball bounced on the rim . . . and went in! The Wheelies won, 64 to 62!

At the emergency room, the doctor said that Tommy's leg was not broken, but he had torn a muscle in the knee, which would take some time to heal.

"It will mean being in a wheelchair for a while," the doctor told him. "How do you feel about that?"

Thinking of Adam, Tommy turned to the doctor, shrugged, and said, "I'll just get on with it."

The following Monday morning, Tommy was sitting in his wheelchair at home, thinking about everything that had happened. He decided that it had all been worth it, even the accident. After all, he'd raised nearly one thousand dollars. Even Mr. Dent had handed over his *one* dollar. But Tommy had decided to frame that. He was sure that the school wouldn't mind.

He lost his train of thought when a horn sounded outside. Ten minutes later he was on the hydraulic platform on the side of the shiny new minibus.

"Tommy, my man!" Adam said, greeting his friend. Turning to everyone else on the bus, he called out, "Everybody, this is Tommy, our new Wheelie!"

The rest of the Wheelies greeted him as the driver started up the engine—this time with no smoke or sputtering—and took off down the street.

"Not only that," Adam continued, "but without his coaching, I wouldn't have been able to make that last shot that won us the game."

Tommy was slightly embarrassed by the cheers and clapping the Wheelies gave him, so he quickly said, "Well, if it wasn't for Adam, I wouldn't have been able to run those one hundred laps and raise money for this new minibus!"

Tommy smiled at his friend, then added, "And I have to admit, riding like this sure beats running for the bus!"